BOLD & EASY
COLORING BOOK

FLOWERS IN ORIGINAL POTS

This book belongs to:

Funny Aura

• • •

Thank you for purchasing our book, we hope you enjoy it! We value feedback from our customers and would love to hear from you. If you have a moment, please consider leaving a review. Thank you!

Take your colors and let's get to it!

THANK YOU FOR MAKING IT THIS FAR

Would you like to receive 30 additional drawings for free? It's easy: simply send an email to **funnyaurapublishing@gmail.com** with your name and email address. Don't forget to write **'POTS'** in the subject line. We will send you the drawings right away so you can keep expressing your creativity!

We really appreciate the time you have taken to enjoy our book. As a publishing house that has just been born, we are very pleased that you have trusted us for your moments of relaxation.

So if you have 50 seconds, we'd love to read your opinion of this book on Amazon.

We'd like to read what this book has brought you!

To leave your review:

1. Open your phone's camera.
2. Bring the phone with the camera closer to this QR.
3. The review page will appear in your browser.